Hope

Hope

Hope Writia

Kapitel 1: Humankind

THE CIRCLE

Every day I hear the universe sing in my ear and the death breathing in my neck. Every day I see the sorrow as a blackness running down of the humanlanes.

But with every single breath I take, I still hope, even when I dont see it, that there will be a day with balance, kindness and forgiveness.

I dont always see the rest, but keep burning in your chest and my fire for you, still dancing every night in my dreams, cause I know we have been travel together in many, many lifes and tried to fullfilment the balance in the world and the question is: If we loose, will that be a winning in its self, so mankind can carry on?

Or if we win, then what? Will the circle come to an end or will it be like ring in the waters from a stone?

But who told you?

But to wish others pain just because you felt the same way is not information, so maybe when you describe the feeling with the same words heals you both yourself and the world, while you at the moment paints a whole new world and right there you where raised from greater depths and found yourself in a changed environment, perhaps a new society, with the second sensed reality with the same colors, the same rubble, panels and ceilings. The grass smells the same way and feels alive under your feet and the people walking around you act human, they cry, feel, think and laugh.

But who told you you were a humanbeing? Was it the world? And if the world can define you and your life, why can't you tell the world who you are? Why not go back into an reflected form, reset and completely without the elongated branches that once stretched over time and collected a precipice teeming with life, but what life? What do you see?

Hope I

Time is not linear, it is part of a subjective process where all the fragments are collective areas of consciousness, the peripheral of a now and then.

Think of tranquility as an ocean, think of your cells as the same substance as a rock you play with. Everything has a beginning, a course and an end, but notice the word everything, there you find it in your heart inside the cell.

Keep in mind that in order to stay in constant well-being it requires collaboration and cohesion, but the overview and calmness you lack, you find only by looking inward and calmly reminding your cells to lovingly re-find the balance of time, tell each cell in your body, that their little wonderful life is a miracle, because without their life you would not exist.

You will probably ask yourself in this home-life who you are? Look inward, maybe you will find the answer in which way you should go, then everything will gather you and everything in you became like all the drops in the same ocean around you. The sea of the many people who are as much you as you are, yet so separate.

Remember to embrace it, the little eternal now.

Hope II

What if this situation startet with a nightmare, then maybe a dream, where there ones opon a time was someone who made a map and drawed this world inside a world. The biggest work ever both with T-cells and blood running like a river in the veins, that was encouraged to carry the life on and on in eternal circles and proces running in different-like painted eyes and personality, the duality between the t-cells and x/y-kromosoms was so much alive.

But what if we forgot the map? What if we forgot that we both are gods and humans? But to bring the life to another proces we have to tell the t-cells the reason why we have to carry on, why we think we deserve to take the one step and start a hole new dream with so much life.

Remember when you start something new from the bottom, that maybe you are the universe and the universe you, and every single movements you made brings the movements to the life beside you and that life beside you feel and act like a reaction to your reaction and in that way you pay it forward, so why not give a little hope and smile to the ones beside you? Why not when your alone, tell your t- cells that every little piece of you matters and the world cannot carry on without you?

Maybe tell a little fairytale about hope!

Your passion

Maybe are the things we use to do sometimes a pain for us we build around and we feel caught in it without knowing that theres opportunities in every choise we make.

If only we could get back our passion for our strengt and talents and the love for glittery and shine, the balustre of the way we act, stand and the way we actually live.

Im not perfect, I dont always see good things in life and I can fail, but I also have bright times and days.

But both you and I can have days that turns to night inside your head and that changes your gravity in that moment you feel the blackness, but hey... Remember that inside that really fucked up place where all your sorrow and madness grows, inside that theres a humanbeing with the idea about how they want to live and the hope for every- thing in every moves they make.

Like a river in my veins

I once traveled across the ocean and found a holy place, inside that place I found you and we laughed and loved each-other for a while but a storm seperated us and since the crash we have been so long away that even the eternity feels like a minut beside and in every breath I take it reminds about a hole world that slipped outside my hands

And the time, oh the time is like a running river and life is outside the door but what about this holy magic there is like a dancing fire when you turn around and look at me?

Where shall I lay my tears? I have so many tears that I think I could build a bridge so you could found home to me and the darkness. Let my try wash it away with a little dash a hope, but to have that hope I need you

Outside my window the rain whisper it again and again

Come to me and bring me back to life, then I'll bring hope back to the world

Once I traveled across the ocean and I try to remember that moment but the days is trying to wash away the memories about you and im not sure I know where to found you anymore

14 *Like a river in my veins*

Even though all my love is lying like a river in my veins

Show me the sun

If you take me to the stars

on a dark night, then I will follow you till the end and I won't regret any moment.

There must be a day where I can reignite.

Show me the sun, I dream about this hollow magic, where you fight for your wings, inside those your strength hiding, follow up the sun in your face.

Dont you see it? The light is allover us

We become the hope in that moment where we both lose faith, but also those days where we raised up to higher depths. Long time ago I saw you on a dark night, there was a light who remind me about the moon, it was like a beautiful nightmare where the darkness turns into inspiration

I followed the burning words in your footsteps. I saw you're light, the basic of your soul. Your whispered to me "Be your own revolution, step inside life and dance. Can't you see it?

You must seize the chance!"

If you take me to the stars on a dark night, then I will follow you till the end and I won't regret any moment, there must be a day where I can reignite my inner sunlight, will you be my light in that story?

I know you already are

Did I see you there in the forest?

I was almost there, at the top of the stairs, with a promise, a sun in a cup. Life woke me up, telling me of a change of plans. Did I see you there in the forest? Did you tell me something?

Was it really you that woke me up, with the sun in your mouth? Dream on, dream on little human. As the days flies past, I loose my grasp of reality, loosing myself in the sun. As my vision moves from the sun towards you. Dreams are fused to my vision by its rays.

Never leaving my sight!

I touch the bottom of the sea constantly to find a footing, what is your purpose? Where is the bearing? I walk in a still wanderer. I wonder about big and small and hear the voice of the sea in your sky by a being.

The roads keep crossing in a still play, quite leisurely, the mirror does not shy away from the truth. The wind, where did you not whisper? You had a voice that reached my toes. I forgot the time and place.

Remember to save the secrets of the sea and your constant speech and silence into one

The night vaults now, twilight is born in a soft eye, bless this beginning of a morning

that rises again as a heat that rolls up and envelops everything to blazing sun. Do you see the same world like I do? See the fight, the light, the dreams and fire? The nightmare allways horrible, but there's a way out there and the morning say hi to you

So hi world

Ode to all the messheads

You are flighty and messy, but in the same chaos you show bravely that you are who you are. You fall for greedy creditors who tempt you with easy money, but at the same time you show that you are as rough and decadent as a diamond. It's okay, through temptation and the mistakes you make, you learn day by day.

You are never at peace and your days end in hyperman-style restless nights, but in reality you know that if you stand still it becomes harder to develop over time and you are sharp enough to know that you have a better chance of to survive if you move, put on the yes hat and let yourself dance into all the challenges, because they are the ones that make you live a little more, just remember to breathe, look at your surroundings and listen.

You linger, you fade, you drown and grief is your companion, but your tears reflect both yourself and your reality and you know the recovery result of that. You are clumsy, drop things, others laugh at you, yet you keep going because you know why.

Gravity cancels you out, yet you're still here.

You are furious and destructive because you are reacting to the way others treated you, but your rage is still therapy, just remember to breathe and see that in your storm you are the learning itself.

You feel excluded and discarded and in your anxiety of losing you forget to make room for the other, but you still have a card you can draw and it is called "Let go"

The disease raging across the world right now, which is nothingness itself, is really time.

It is here to remind you that everything has a beginning, a process and an end, but even if exactly THAT process ends, remember that it starts again, but within that process, so remember that time itself both is eternity, but also the one asking you to continue what you came here for and finish the process properly. We are all a snapshot and you my friend can still manage to pass on your moment.

The years that flew by in a great whirlwind

The pain prys out and in between the nerves and underneath rests the liquid inflammatory mass, which perhaps also bears witness to never-healed wounds over time. The years that flew by in a great whirlwind of chaos and orthodox platitudes with bottled emptiness, the melted words that shaped my whole life. They danced up and down, side by side with the question of faith and existential questions.

"Our body is made up of 90% water, maybe water really IS the source of life? So if I drown in tears, am I not dehydrated?"

In a world filled with nightmares spread across the news, anxiety dances on a tightrope in intervals while the world still stands and calls, sighs and burns. I look again and again at the soaked ground, the tears from the sky and the sun desperately and hungrily eating the curtains to reach me.

I know how it feels. It thirsts, hungers and screams for visibility, while we all walk around blind, just as lost and alone as it... But my body is a temple and it contains all the sounds and the images. The question is whether I am sinking or actually rising because I feel and sense the world so intensely that I CAN do nothing but recognize that I am actually alive.

Kapitel 2: Life in another form

Wordstorm

In all sorts of crooked angles and edges, I was convinced I knew you from another life. You have been right under my skin, stored my days, like letters written all over me and inside. I remembered you as a dark road where the light only just broke through, the darkness was my own self-tormented temple. I have fought so many battles, seen so many things and been to many places, but in everything I did I was looking for you. When I finally found you, the whole picture changed. Why live without you when you illuminate the whole picture just by being present? Out of the fog you came, you led me out, everything continued, your individual was the comma I was missing

And now I continue

I see you scratch yourself up in front of me like a graying reality, images wander in and out of that door with the many memories and fragments. I think of how you said goodmorning to the world with a smile, while the smile broke the many constellations into a thousand pieces, and then gathered it all back into one big whole, when your being, whispered how real your smile really was. Why even try to put it in other words? But the words continue to haunt you, while I wallow in a wordstorm myself.

Tender about life

The illusions wait outside my window, while I desperately feel the tipping inward of my lingering temple and I rummage around in several constellations of time, dreams and zig-zagging heady nightmares with the spiritual that so softly and intensely tries to roam me right there.

Somewhere among the stars I find myself in a desolate room, pensive, lingering, and tender about life, while I still try to unravel all the riddles, hang my whole life out to dry with still images and all the reflections that are on the line when you unorthodoxly trying to teach me to spin the magic songs of wisdom.

In just a little over 11 hours you'll round off and tell me I'm your witch goddess, eternal bride of darkness and I'm sinking down, down into distant oval depths as I try to find my footing, call myself up to the mist of lifeworld. The world I so burningly live, breathe and speak for when I dance that dance inside your gaze.

The dance that draws the entire map of your oval heart's dreams.

Dear Luna

I heard your whisper the other day, in the form of a letter. I saw the promising green leaves as a call to me. They were like letters, but completely abstract and blurred like the Aarhus tidal sea. I felt your breath like a whisper in my hair, you understood playing like children in coal buckets and tinkling laughter. I knew your smile, like the white springday you were. I knew your movements, which in those times looked into my soul with that eye which all and no one knew. Barresso's nostalgic mind called to me with coffee drinks, a touch of springmusic and life, but life around the corner came dancing with writerly smiles and the memories that poured through that door. The song of spring kept dancing.

When I went to Aarhus street, you were with me. When I went down to The Permanent I felt it so deeply: The summer that came storming like the horseman of the light, sailed past me with long bright hours outstretched in one hand.

To memory of my dead writerfriend Louise Bach

Life

Can you scream for me?
Can you be that moment I left?

One morning I Saw you in the forest and I drowned in the obscure lust for dreams. I wanted to tell you that I liked the shadow in your eyes, your way that you actually lived, and the hope for us today, is that every moment can be alive and not broken.

I saw U the other day and wanted to touch you, you were my world, the day I left yesterday. Why do you keep me away, when I want more? The day is my prioritet and I love the moves, the smell and risle in the wind. Where do I go now? I try everyday to fit in, to have my own life and my dreams keep telling me that I have a bright future, but in eternal light.

Do you know my light? In my dreams you are a like a

dangerous, mysterious wild child, that keep burning in my chest, will you rest? Where do you want me to go, where to be? Every day I see your light, and you sorrow that hung like a strand from your every single moves and youre trying to telling me something. I know you want to touch and burn, you want to tell me everything and I hope someday we can talk about everything.

Your lips is like a running dayriver and a dream is hiding in your eyes, like a wild flower. Do you see what I want to learn you? My way to act, my way to telling you stories and hint beside the rolling doors, is my way to handle you.

Life, you like a dream to me, keep burning for me, keep hope in my days, lie the prays down on my pillow and stay there in a silence eternity.

The eternity that flew by

Looking out over the horizon as light and shadow change, I count the days that all at once transform into a panoramic scream as you wander in and out of that door. In my hands I carry the answer to you. You wanted to separate from me: “I am you, you are me” But the veins that flew by dragged eternity with them, while your comma continued to pursue my period. I know I'm too intense but expect nothing, the past leaves behind me as I hear your whisper. The speech of the wind, unnoticed singing little haiku verses, the days that stroll over my head, days of time. I come to life in the middle of a dream, wild and motley I run towards red, while the whole past tumbles behind me. The sun is quietly beating down on me.

In my eyes, Einstein's theory of relativity is like an energy that cooperates to create unity. The very power of human thought only has power if the thought itself carries the strength and the strength is born from your belief that it can be done.

The mirror

My whole life has been full of strange events. I have danced on my 19th birthday on top of a speaker in a brandert on Train. I have cried at Vesterport station in Copenhagen. I have sat and listened to a priest's sexlife in the train towards the unknown, although he was probably not a priest as he claimed.

When my sister gave birth to her first child, I was reminded of how fragile life is. I have walked through many dark corridors, changed and could not recognize myself, the mirror's composure was unbearable, the face of time whispered to me. Hardly had I closed a door before a window opened, quietly I took the first step, left everything behind and soared towards the horizon where life waited, but the white edge of the stars, is sharply cut, it is with utter amazement that I recognize it . That life is open floodgates, sometimes as I traveled in the consciousness of my soul, I came to the word. After years of silence, I learned to speak. Communicating with the world is not only important, but a life ingredient for me, but a recipe everyone can and should use.

I became whole.

Dualistic world

That thing about life... What is it? I always thought there was a meaning to everything, but suddenly I stop, the tide has receded. The faded footprints are only faintly visible now, as if I'm walking around in a parallel world, in a dualistic society, call it what you will, but there are two sides to this world. The inner and the outer. Unfortunately, I seem to wake up to an outside world. That can't quite fit, can it? Where did the depth go? Gravity?

My silence approaches a shout, my movements approach violent behavior, as if with my violent movements and silent screams I want to say something, but my words are meaningless objects. In due time I flew out on the silent surface of the tide. Stared at me blindly, in an underground current where the depth reaches further down than we humans would ever reach in our consciousness.

I just know that I have been there before, and many

places I have been, many people I have known.

Thoughtstreak

I am here, where I want to be. And not to forget - I got here myself. Like a butterfly on the move, I flutter around, and the sound of the fire of hearts, smacks on the tongue. I grow into the light, slowly, movingly, wisps of thought.

My body is of a brighter point in the center of your intense vulnerability, yes you. It's you I'm talking to. Listen to me, my words, or just the silence that dances around, right where I stand. I know that once you would talk, laugh and look into my eyes. Uncertainly, I grope my way forward, at the top of my mind in convoluted rhythms I mindfuck the spring. And the sun walks across the city's roofs, telling stories and stories. Happy rays dance the fandango and I live. Isn't that the most important thing? The past rolls backwards.

And I speak and time passes, I have lost my footing for a time. But right now I know where I want to go and I love life. Period.

Rethink

When I was little I always wondered where we came from, a little voice in my ear whispered: Why are we here? How did the universe originate? My love for life was infinite and my wonder great. I could spend many hours walking around nature, where I felt and sensed everything up close. To some extent, I was more present then than I am now, when Facebook was invented and all kinds of worries etched into my brain. We have built surfaces so strong and robust that it is difficult to break out. Everything has become so digitized that we are almost living in a Matrix.

Why are we here? Whispered the voice again.

We are lost creatures trapped by the zeitgeist. Slaves of the unimportant. If we talked more about what we have lost, we might find it again. Instead, no one speaks, flat consonants fall to the ground. Do we want our next generations to pass nothing on?

Go for a walk in the world and look around, feel the deep sun. The rays crawl on tiptoe over houses, gardens and roads, it has a story and its mission is to enlighten. See how the world is like a shadow dance. Now the low sun is your bearing, your sailing in life. Do what you feel and dream about, don't be afraid.

Why are we here? I whispered.

www.ingramcontent.com/pod-product-compliance
Lightning Source LLC
LaVergne TN
LVHW080356180826
845678LV00025B/1758

* 9 7 8 8 7 9 9 5 4 5 5 4 4 *